LOVE
END LOST JESUS DEAD
HELP FUTURE IDENTITY GOD
TURN CLEANERS ANSWER DAWN
TOGETHER QUESTIONS GET SELFISH
LORD SUMMERTIME
SUMMERTIME CLAM PRISONER
FAILURE
JOURNEY BASKETBALL
EYE DUSK SEARCH SALESMAN POET
FIELD FOUND FRIEND
LIFE CALL STARE

# Lost & Found
## André Lodrée

Printed in the United States of America
First Printing, 2013
ISBN 0-9858658-1-4

Published by André Lodrée

I dedicate this book to my wife, Candice, my daughters, Nichele & Layla, and my son, André III, they are my motivation and inspiration in everything I do and every choice I make. I also dedicate this to my parents and grandparents, who always supported me and made me who I am today.

*Thank You*

# Contents

## Found

# Lost

# Selfish

*"Let nothing be done through strife or vainglory; but in lowliness of mind let each esteem other better than themselves."*
Philippians 2:3(KJV)

The flower emerges
With the sun's continuous surges
The water falls
And answers the flower's call
The flower needs the light and water
They are the flower's mother and father

The beginning of life begins
Where is the end?
The people of the world must answer
Answer what?
The call

Many say there is a call of the wild
A call of the free
A call of the brave and courageous
A call of the unique
A call of the intelligent
Which one do we answer?

People spend most of their life pleasing others
Whether it is their sisters, fathers, brothers, or mothers
What about yourself

# Search

*"Because strait is the gate, and narrow is the way, which leadeth unto life, and few there be that find it."*
Matthew 7:14(KJV)

The man has been lost for years
His family has come to me with many tears
I feel their pain
And I have been on the case through snow and rain

I've looked for him in his old neighborhood
I've searched for him in his old school
I've searched for him in his new neck of the woods
Is he right under my nose, I'm such a fool

He was my best friend
When we were in class he knew all the answers
When I wanted to kick it he made me do the right thing
Now that he is gone I'm lost in this world

I'm trying to be a good detective
But he is hidden to deep
Steadily pushed further down everyday I sleep
Who is this kidnapper, he is very destructive

Help me find him!
He is the answers to all my questions
He is the ideas to all my suggestions
Help me find him!

The search continues . . .

# The Field

*"Behold the fowls of the air: for they sow not, neither do they reap, nor gather into barns; yet your heavenly Father feedeth them. Are ye not much better than they?"*
Matthew 6:26(KJV)

The wind is blowing every which and way
Is the sun coming out today?
I am surrounded by a world
Everything is blurred
The field

I see a bird flying low
Looking for a worm
Where he was going to find one I don't know
As I take my eyes off the bird I see a worm on a fern
The field

The worm spots the bird and begins to take cover
The bird sees the worm and hovers
Toward the worm, the worm dives in the hole
I wonder will the bird try to take his soul
The field

The bird snatches the worm by its tail
The bird flies to his nest and fed her child
All the while I hear the worm's soul yell
The bird's child sees the worm and smiles
The field

The bird is satisfied
The child's hunger has been fulfilled
The worm is dead
The bird's child was fed
The battlefield

# The Journey

*"Rise ye up, take your journey, and pass over the river Arnon: behold, I have given into thine hand Sihon the Amorite, king of Heshbon, and his land: begin to possess it, and contend with him in battle."*
Deuteronomy 2:24(KJV)

I am searching for something
I have not discovered what it is
I will struggle with this probably for the rest of my life
I wish I could solve this problem in a day

Many people say I look unprofessional
Is it because I know how to have a good time?
Is it because I joke around a lot?
Is it because I love my frat?
Is it because I'm never seen as serious?
I'm tired of trying to mold myself into what people want

I love playing basketball
I love my frat
I love to joke around
I love to go to parties
The best job is doing what you love to do best

But I have neglected a side of me I want to share
A side that likes going to class
A side that likes to study
A side that likes to write
A side that enjoys school
Can I do what I love and go to school?

In order for me to succeed I must conform
But isn't individuality the best
Would I still be an individual if I do what other people want?

# Clam

*"Again, the kingdom of heaven is like unto a merchant man, seeking goodly pearls: Who, when he had found one pearl of great price, went and sold all that he had, and bought it."*
Matthew 13:45-46(KJV)

I've been around the world
Let me stop lying, psst I haven't even been close
But I've been chasing around for the clam that holds my pearl
And searching for the pen that can write my quotes

I guess I need that one thing to put me over my humps
The thing that can give me air time like MJ when he dunks
I think I should have found it by now
But I'm stuck in this foolish circus like an old clown

Sometimes
I think I catch a glimpse
Then somebody rolls up a window with all type a tint
Maybe that somebody is me
Maybe I'm scared to let my ambitions be free

What I got to be scared of?
Not receiving no love
Getting cut from the main event
Then realizing I'm just an average simp

Wasn't I raised to surpass this
And not just succumb to bum bliss
My parents taught me to look fear in the eyes
And take the devil by surprise

I've been around the world
Let me stop lying, psst I haven't even been close
But I've been chasing around for the clam that holds my pearl
Hey there goes some rocks maybe it's under those?

I've been around the block
Plucked hundreds of clams with no pearls

Psst, I'm not even close


## Stare

*"Look unto me, and be ye saved, all the ends of the earth: for I am God, and there is none else."*
Isaiah 45:22(KJV)

People stare at me
I catch them sometimes
They do not know what they are staring at or why
People stare at me
Is it my shoes, my hair, my zits
Are people nosy
People stare at me
I look at people and wonder what they are thinking
I guess I stare at them
But people stare at me
When I'm walking down the street
Gangs and my brothers and my sisters stare at me
Is it me, do I act like I'm better than them
I hope not
My people should know that I am the same
If we walk down the street together
People will stare at us both
People stare.

# Lost

*"For the Son of man is come to seek and to save that which was lost."*
Luke 19:10(KJV)

I'm stuck in a jam I can't get out of
It seems I have forgotten what my dream was
Every door I go in I come out the same
Nothing solved, no different feelings, no one to blame
I went to a party, greatest party ever
Every dance seemed like it was going to last forever
DJ playin' jams all night
So many women to choose from, beauty on my left and right
But I went in and came out the same
Nothing solved, no different feelings, no one to blame
Man, I love movies watch them all the time
So many special effects my finger stuck on rewind
And don't forget the dramas I love those too
With a plot so thick I can't see through
Mysteries that are baffling and captivate my mind
Who's the killer, who's guilty, innocent, too late out of time
Out of all the movies I've seen at the end I feel the same
Nothing solved, no questions answered, no one to blame

We kickin' it, we smokin', we drinkin'
Everything to keep from thinking
Man it's fun getting high and drunk and acting a fool
Sayin' to ourselves "We too cool!"
No matter how many drugs I did, I still felt the same
Nothing solved, no questions answered, no one to blame
Sex the root of all my transgressions
Talking about love, when it was just lust and fornication
Women coming and going in and out of my life
Not doing anything but causing me strife
With every woman I wasn't happier just the same
Nothing solved, no love, and only me to blame

# Nightmares

*"Forasmuch then as Christ hath suffered for us in the flesh, arm yourselves likewise
with the same mind: for he that hath suffered in the flesh hath ceased from sin; That
he no longer should live the rest of his time in the flesh to the lusts of men, but to the
will of God."*
1 Peter 4:1-2(KJV)

Memories are like nightmares
Things that the mind thinks are rare
We want to forget the pain and sorrow
Just so we can take a glance into tomorrow
These tomorrows are not promised
And most of the time missed
"I'll do it tomorrow . . ." that's what we say
Knowing yesterday is forgotten everyday
Maybe the pain of yesterday will become sorrow
Should we look at the present?

Yesterday is all we have, maybe the only guarantee
What we have will make our tomorrows be
Remember the time you . . . no, you probably forgot
Why can't you remember when you were young and the joy and fun
never stopped
You might have traveled, went there, did this, and did that
Kicked it with your homies and stepped with your frat
Memories are nightmares cause they show you, you could've
You should've, and you would've
But you didn't
Now you just keep slippin
Knowing you are not where you want to be
Or who you want to be
You need help, look at the past
Because that's what you should've did last
And maybe what you should do next
And drop the drugs, drinking, and sex
You messed up, you can never make it right?
Never say never without a fight

Come with me to a new tomorrow

Where you can turn your memories into dreams

## The Dead End

*"If my people, which are called by my name, shall humble themselves, and pray, and seek my face, and turn from their wicked ways; then will I hear from heaven, and will forgive their sin, and will heal their land."*
2 Chronicles 7:14(KJV)

The road is ending
Will we see a turn somewhere

We are going down a dead end
Do we not see the signs
What is wrong with our minds
People come together so we can start to round this bend

The road is ending
Will we see a turn somewhere

We need a new road
Maybe, a rainbow with a pot of gold
What is the answer, does anyone know?
Are they my friends or foes?

The road is ending
Will we see a turn up ahead

Black, white, yellow, green, they're just colors
What about me and you?
Different colors, are we not still sisters and brothers?
Maybe only God can help us through

The road is ending
Will we see a turn ahead

We must become one
Without this, this world is done
People must evaluate themselves

Put their hatred, distrust, racism on the shelves

The road is ending
We must find a turn


# The Future

As I walk through the world
I see it changing and destroying
My older family members remember when the world was a pearl
They say how people been toying
With God's land and souls
Although my family members are old
I know they speak the truth
Because the movie scenes and books also told
These great stories of old telephone booths, old automobiles, old homes, and old radios
Is old better?
Is history going to repeat itself?
These answers are hard to find, just like predicting tomorrow's weather
When we get old we will be able to tell our stories
We will say how bus rides use to be a dollar and fifty cents
We will tell stories of our days of glory
How we could buy a pop for sixty-five cents
We are the future we need to make the future
The future should be better, not worst

# Life

*"O ye sons of men, how long will ye turn my glory into shame? how long will ye love vanity, and seek after leasing? Selah."*
Psalm 4:2(KJV)

This is the longest race I've ever ran
It seems like it ain't gonna ever end
I see my teammate, my best friend
There's my mom, my favorite fan

I go around a turn, another hurdle
Man I thought I wasn't fertile
I should've been smarter
Maybe God wanted my life to be harder
Hurdle!!

Columbus found America in ?
I knew the answer, but I did not raise my hand
Another test without a pen
I slipped my late homework on the professor's stand
Hurdle, Jump, Fell
Why didn't I see that one coming?
Because I was too busy running
From my success, from my failure, from my expectations
Here comes my grandma with her suggestions
Hurdle, knocked it over

What do I want in life?
When will I do what's right!
How will I get through these hard times?
Maybe Jesus will ease my mind?
Hurdle, almost cleared it
I want to finish this race
Not in third, but first place
I want to give God some glory
So I can continue on with my story

There's the finish line

# Poet

I sit and stare
Maybe I think, too
I have to find something to write that's new
Either I do or don't, what do I care

I look in the sky to try and find something there
I look at rocks on the earth
Or maybe the mother's new birth
I look in my heart for something dear

I live for tomorrow to find
A phenomenon that blows my mind
I search for it forever
I look for the writings on the wall in stormy weather

I listen to a heartbeat
Or the patter of baby's feet
I listen to the engine of a car
I listen to the mind of a superstar

I watch television to see the stereotypes
But if I watch too long I couldn't tell wrong from right
I watch the stars twinkle
I listen to the guitar strings fiddle

But I just glance at life

# Identity

*"I will rise now, and go about the city in the streets, and in the broad ways I will seek him whom my soul loveth: I sought him, but I found him not."*
Song of Solomon 3:2(KJV)

I look and try to find
But what am I looking for?
Is it life, money or popularity?
I don't know but I need to find it

It's important and essential
When I find it, it will benefit me
I can look and look forever
However I'm running out of time

The world is ending
My brothers and sisters are dying
But I'm still looking
Hurry up they need me

Why can't I find this
Is it because I do not recognize it
Don't stop looking, keep looking
Where is it, I don't know

Wait you're looking for it, too?
Do you know what it is?
I need to know

It's me

# The Turn

*"Who is he that overcometh the world, but he that believeth that Jesus is the Son of God?"*

1 John 5:5(KJV)

As I sit and stare
I wonder if the world will turn
It is as though wondering was a dare
Because the world is lives and burns
The world still turns

Black vs White
Wrong vs Right
Majority vs Minority
Segregation vs Unity
Yet the world still turns

It is as though the people do not care
They kill, steal, drink, lust, and sleep
They waste money on expensive clothes to wear
Then a telephone rings or a beeper beeps
Then the world continues to turn

The end is near, will the world end?
People say yes
Are they trying to get money or give the world something to believe
in?
The world will soon be over this year at least
The world does not stop

A child is shot on the corner
The chalk is there in the morning
Someone rapes a woman and burns her
The ashes are there in the evening
The world still turns

Our lives are changed everyday
The moon is blue and the sun is yellow
Many get paid on Friday

The man decided to kill a nice fellow
The world is turning even faster

This massacre must end
Today and tomorrow
We must become friends
We must love each other and be someone to follow
The world will . . . . . .


## Summertime

*"Yea, though I walk through the valley of the shadow of death, I will fear no evil:
for thou art with me; thy rod and thy staff they comfort me."*
Psalm 23:4 (KJV)

The bus stops
I get off as fast as I can
Why?
It is a matter of respect for fellow riders
As I cross the street
I see these girls at least fourteen
One has her short dress on
Trying hard to be a woman
Her friend has daisy dukes on
They both got weave
They call these girls hood rats

I continue walking
I see a barricade of sprinklers on
I have to time the sprinklers so I won't get wet
I don't want to run on the grass
When I get pass the sprinklers I see the park
The folks gang run this park and this territory

As I continue to walk I notice the cracks
I trip over one and try to play it off
I glance and see a brother coming by
He looks like a thug
I put my head down, never look up

It was fear
I was afraid of this thug or gang banger
No, I was afraid of myself

# Questions

*"Who shall change our vile body, that it may be fashioned like unto his glorious body, according to the working whereby he is able even to subdue all things unto himself."*
Philippians 3:21(KJV)

My world is now
I am in a circus
I am the clown
Everyone is trying to get on my bus
But is this bus going downtown?

I see this girl
She is the most beautiful thing in the world
I will marry her tomorrow
I'm not a good man 'cause I don't understand her sorrow
Is this bus going downtown?

I hit a bump, it was a basketball
I look in the rearview mirror the kid is crying
I go back to give the kid some money for the ball
I pick up the damaged ball and kept driving
Where's the bus going?

Mrs. Dantzler!! Where have you been?
She looks at me and says "Where are you going?"
I was astonished and knew my dream could not be seen
My head was clear and I began moving
My bus is going up town

# Salesman

*"I have gone astray like a lost sheep; seek thy servant; for I do not forget thy commandments."*
Psalm 119:176(KJV)

I gave everything I had
I put my life on the line for nothing
I was following a fad
I was chasing the girls, the fame, the bling
And as I sat in the chair I thought
What did I gain?
I looked at my life in disgust
I didn't have the girls, the bling or the fame
My life was a bust
I owe my family, credit cards, bills and tickets
This fad had become my life
And now I can't fix this
This life has caused me nothing but strife

At that moment I heard a knock
As I inquired "Who is it?"
The voice replied, "It is I."
I didn't recognized the voice
But he sounded as if he knew me, I had no choice
I had to ask, "Where do I know you from?"
"I'm an old friend." He replied
As he talked I began to recognize
I tried to look out the window to see him
But the trees were blocking him
I remembered don't talk to strangers
But something on the inside comforted my sense of danger

As he tried to remind me of our experiences
My heart and soul began to ignore my mind's differences
My mind was saying he is a thief coming for you
But I have nothing, so what is he here to do
My mind said he is a door-to-door salesman
So I said "I don't care if you do know me I'm not buying what you are selling!"

17

"I don't want to sale you anything I want to give you something."
What does he have to give me I don't deserve anything?
My mind said he's probably going to try and kill you
Then he said, "I come that you might have life and that you might
have it more abundantly."

When he said that I believed and opened the door
As the door opened I fell to the floor
He helped me up and held me in his arms –
"Look no further . . . ."

# *Found*

# Get Together

*"And when they had found him, they said unto him, All men seek for thee."*
Mark 1:37(*KJV*)


Love, peace, and happiness I been looking
From women to cars to good cooking
Everywhere I look is wrong
Different music, same song
There it was the answer to all my questions – Church

I'm going, meeting new people and new friends
Some old saints sayin' "Where you been?"
My answer blank
After church I began to think
Where have I been?
I have spent my last years
Going no where and holding back more tears
I mean look at my accomplishments

Wait, what accomplishments
I don't have any of those
I met a girl, I proposed
We broke up and that hurt
I went to basketball tryouts saying "This time it's going to work!"
Never made it, no experience, not good enough
Mama said life was tough

I had three cars none lasted that long
I'm stuck in the 80s, what am I doing wrong?
I had a beautiful, Kool-Aid smile daughter
But I couldn't succeed at being an at home father
My life is filled with separation, failure and lust
Getting my life together is a must

# Doing

*"Knowing that whatsoever good thing any man doeth, the same shall he receive of the Lord, whether he be bond or free."*
Ephesians 6:8(KJV)

I sit back to enjoy life and all it's goodness
I see the past that I've been through with all my mess
I see the near death experiences that I caused
I see the drugs and alcohol
What did I do?

I remember the fornication and the disobedience of your word
I notice all the different gods I served
From parties, to women, to money, and more
All of these I embraced, but Jesus I ignored
What did I do?

I was wrong and sinning against God
But the more I sinned the more I felt odd
I knew what I was doing was wrong and did not care
But for some reason Jesus was still there
What will I do?

I was lost in the maze of this world
Thinking it was the money, the cars, apparel
I began to question my decision
And I knew and he knew it was not apart of his vision
What did I do?

I was searching, looking for an escape
But I continued to hear the same tape
I should've, I could've, I would've
What did I do?

My life in this world was over and a new life he started
And with that devil I parted
He was mad, but Jesus was glad
What did I do, to deserve such love and mercy

I did nothing of good as far as I could see
But Jesus, but Jesus he died for me.
What will I do?

# I Call

*"His name shall endure for ever: his name shall be continued as long as the sun: and men shall be blessed in him: all nations shall call him blessed."*
Psalm 72:17(*KJV*)

Jesus, I call you glory!

You give me wisdom and understanding to do better in my life. As I embrace you I receive a new life, a new way.

Jesus, I call you joy!

Peace and happiness you gave me with your life. As you call me I run in that direction.

Jesus, I call you love!

They stabbed you in your side and you died. How could you sacrifice yourself, your life for little old me.

Jesus, I call you strength!

As trials and tests come upon me you lift me up and carry me through. And as I get weaker and weaker you get stronger and stronger in me.

Jesus, I call you faith!

You are my hero. You complete every step I take and believe every move I make is for you.

Jesus, I call you family!

My father you are. You give me advice and visions of your path.

Jesus, I call you grace!

Even when my life was walking away from you, every time I tripped you caught me. You made my fall that much softer.

Jesus, I call you Jesus!

You are my savior, the only one I adore. I look to you for all answers.

Jesus, I say thank you!

## The Answer

*"Hear me speedily, O LORD: my spirit faileth: hide not thy face from me, lest I be like unto them that go down into the pit."*
Psalm 143:7(KJV)

Lord you answered
I was out there alone with no friend
No one to trust in
Enemy was around me on every side
But I wouldn't turn to you because of pride
I lived as though I was running from you
But your love still shined through
My days were numbered my end was coming
But I kept running

As I ran you showed me the things I was running from
My family, your love, your blessings, I was dumb
You gave me a plan for my life when I was young
But I was convinced that living for you wasn't fun
Can't do this, can't do that, can't go here, can't go there

Where?
Where was I going? What was I doing?
Nothing

I was taring myself down with my evil ways
Your love was not phased
You were focused on me
Even though I continued to flee
Then something happened I lost my breath
My body, my soul needed a rest

So I stopped, hands on my knees
Life without you was a tease
A minute of happiness, a second of pleasure
All that running with nothing to measure
I wasn't successful in life
Only pain and strife
I looked back at all the things I ran from
I saw where I belonged and it was fun

Lord I know I've been going in the wrong direction
Looking for material pleasures and fleshly affection
I turned my back on you and your plan
But now here I stand
Ready to go forward in your will
Ready to be filled
I need the Holy Ghost in my life to lead and guide
To subject my will, my way, my pride
As I began to take my first step to run back to Jesus
Thinking Jesus or bust
You appeared before me
No need to run I've always been with you


## Basketball

*"Restore unto me the joy of thy salvation;
and uphold me with thy free spirit."*
Psalm 51:12(*KJV*)

Beneath the air as a gift
Bend knees, let your blood flow
Let the world go

24

Focus, focus, focus
Time is a-wasting
Take a deep breath
Let it come to you
Release, release, release
The tension has gone away
You are free, free, free . . . .


## Cleaners

*"But if we walk in the light, as he is in the light, we have fellowship one with another, and the blood of Jesus Christ his Son cleanseth us from all sin."*
1 John 1:7*(KJV)*

People running everyday, to get where?
Everywhere, anywhere, and no where
How bout jogging, speed walkin'
Maybe even a little struntin'
Y'all be tryin' the fast and short way
Who said the cleaner's service in one day
Are better than the cleaner's regular service
Take your time cleaners with my clothes
I ain't in no rush

You say
She says
He says
Who's report will I believe
The king of kings or the prince of thieves
Take your time cleaners with my clothes
I ain't in no rush

The world is movin' fast
But whatever they been doin', they been doin' since the past
Shoot, I'm lookin' for somethin' new
Cleaners! Take your time with my clothes
I ain't in no rush

Love! Don't nobody love me and you, that's what I said

But somebody gave me God's word and I read and read
There it is as clear as day he died on the cross for you and me
Why and how did he know I was part of his destiny?
He put his faith in me before I gave up my sins
My love, my heart, my soul I give to Jesus my friends
Jesus! Jesus! Take your time with my soul
Shape me, mold me, and make me whole
I ain't in no rush

## Lord

*"To the end that my glory may sing praise to thee, and not be silent. O LORD my God, I will give thanks unto thee for ever."*
Psalm 30:12(KJV)

Thank you Lord
I say, thank you Lord!

You're my healer
My protector
My way maker, oh yeah!!

Thank you Lord
I say, thank you Lord!

You're my savior
My answer
My director, oh yeah!!

Thank you Lord
I say, thank you Lord!
Thank you Lord
I say, thank you Lord!

# Lord's Help

*"I can do all things through Christ which strengtheneth me."*
Philippians 4:13(KJV)

I can do the impossible with the help from the Lord
I can reach the unreachable with the help from the Lord
I can think the unthinkable with the help from the Lord

I can do all things with the help from the Lord
I can do all things with the help from the Lord

I can soar like an eagle with the help from the Lord
I can do my dreams with the help from the Lord
I can do my best with the help from the Lord

I can do all things with the help from the Lord
I can do all things with the help from the Lord

My blinded eyes can see with the help from the Lord
I can be me with the help from the Lord
I can be free with the help from the Lord

I can do all things with the help from the Lord
I can do all things with the help from the Lord
I can do all things with the help from the Lord
I can do all things with the help from the Lord

# I Call You

*"The next day John seeth Jesus coming unto him, and saith, Behold the Lamb of God, which taketh away the sin of the world."*
John 1:29(*KJV*)

Jesus I call you, Jesus I call you
Jesus I call you, Jesus I call you

Jesus I call you friend
You know when to step in
Jesus I call you father
You died to take me farther
Jesus I call you king
You are in control of everything

Jesus I call you, Jesus I call you
Jesus I call you, Jesus I call you

Jesus I call you glory
You gave my life a new story
Jesus I call you love
You watch over me from above
Jesus I call you Lord
Your will never be ignored

Jesus I call you, Jesus I call you
Jesus I call you, Jesus I call you
Jesus I call you, Jesus I call you
Jesus I call you, Jesus I call you

# My God

*"And God said unto Moses, I AM THAT I AM: and he said, Thus shalt thou say unto the children of Israel, I AM hath sent me unto you."*
Exodus 3:14(KJV)

God, you are my God
When the earth is famine, you are
When joy has been stolen from me, you are

You've kept me in thick and thin
Your love for me continues to the bitter end
You're on my left, my right, behind me and in front of me
You've done more for me than I can see

God, you are my God
When people laugh at me, you are
When mountains are, you are

You're my thirst, my hunger
Yet you make my days even longer
I do not deserve this love, but you give
Me give? Not then, but now my love for you is exclusive
I enjoy your presence
I can't believe you keep me in your embrace

God, you are my God
When the blizzard has blinded me, you are
When my friends have turned on me, you are

Enemies are attacking without regard
Their blows come fast, quick and bring me down hard
However, the full blow I never feel
Because God you are my force field
Do I strike back? Never
You protecting me is your endeavor
I've never lifted a sword
I only cling to your word
The victory you've given me
With one word you set me free

God, you are my God
The wall is too tall, you are
I cannot move I'm surrounded, you are

I'm a stranger in an unknown land
But yet Father I stand
My home I have never seen
But I know it exist because you say what you mean
You've given glimpses of how good it shall be
Through your blessings you continue to bestow upon me

God, you are my God
Your way you've written in your word, I follow
Your words and promises are not hollow
God, you are my God
Me, I am your son


# Dusk And Dawn

*"The eternal God is thy refuge, and underneath are the everlasting arms: and he shall thrust out the enemy from before thee; and shall say, Destroy them."*
Deuteronomy 33:27(KJV)

My problems seem unbearable
But you have the answers to get me through
And I always know you're able
Lord continue to do what you do

There you are standing with open arms
You are my dusk and dawn
There you are

Jesus you bring the truth to light
You have a perfect plan
Because of you I don't have to fight
My victory is in your hands

There you are standing with open arms

You are my dusk and dawn
There you are

My needs you know them well
And everyday you provide
You are not able to fail
You are my tide come to wash away my pains
You are the rainbow after the rain

There you are standing with open arms
You are my dusk and dawn
There you are

## Failure

*"And what shall I more say? for the time would fail me to tell of Gedeon, and of Barak, and of Samson, and of Jephthae; of David also, and Samuel, and of the prophets: Who through faith subdued kingdoms, wrought righteousness, obtained promises, stopped the mouths of lions."*
Hebrews 11:32-33(KJV)

My Lord and Savior Jesus I have failed
I want to follow hard after your heart, but I stumbled
I turned not to you, but to my own understanding
I've failed

Was this test too hard for me?
If it was, why didn't I look unto thee?
You are the way, the truth, and light of the world
But I did not look to you for a referral
I was trying to please myself
But I said you are my strength and help
I've failed

As I look at my failure, my short comings
I see your grace and forgivings
But I will not hold to this failure, but pursue excellence
I can never be excellent therefore you must give me guidance
If you don't teach me and show me

I will never be

Father you had the same tests
But you still performed your best
You prayed, you studied God's word, and you knew your purpose
So to get to my best I must do this

When the enemy is against me, I must pray
When I am blessed above measure, I must pray
When the devil comes to steal my word, I must read the Bible more
When I've read the Bible front and back, I must read the Bible more
Faced with a problem I can't solve, I must know my purpose
The enemy has been defeated, I must know my purpose

My excellence is only through your grace and mercy
You possess ways and means I can never perceive
My joy and peace, you gave
My life and soul, you paid
You've given so much I can never match
But I gave you my soul, my life, and I will never slack
Every mistake, every misstep I will continue to praise you
I will search for excellence through you
Failing is not my practice
But following your word and pleasing you is my substance
You are my Lord and Savior Jesus
I love you

## Jesus' Love

*"Jesus said unto him, Thou shalt love the Lord thy God with all thy heart, and with all thy soul, and with all thy mind."*
Matthew 22:37(KJV)

He died for you, He died for me
He gave us all liberty
He died for you, He died for me

For this I praise his name
And continue to increase his fame

He died for you, He died for me
He gave us all liberty
He died for you, He died for me

He carried the cross for our sins
I'm saved because of him

He died for you, He died for me
He gave us all liberty
He died for you, He died for me

He had me in his destiny
He gave his life on Calvary
He sent back the comforter

He died for you, He died for me
He saved us all from captivity
He died for you, He died for me
He died for you, He died for me
He gave us all liberty
He died for you, He died for me

## Friend's Prisoner

*"This I say then, Walk in the Spirit, and ye shall not fulfil the lust of the flesh."*
Galatians 5:17(*KJV*)

I must be like a bird in flight
Flying in the sky with my wings breaking through the light
But I cannot go without the wind
A prisoner of my friend
We travel together united in a covenant
That has been formed since time was spent
I have been searching for a new friend
Not so demanding someone who knows how to bend

Don't walk on the grass use the sidewalk

As I look to the sun
I wonder is he the one
So much power in one circle of fire
I know if I want to see him I will be very tired
The travel is much too long for little me
This covenant probably wouldn't set me free

Don't walk on the grass use the sidewalk

Wait what about the moon
I feel like a child watching a cartoon
Excited and laughing with pleasure the band had been broken
The wind stepped in as soon as my words were spoken
The wind blew the moon away
Even after I continued to beckon it to stay
This moon, this sun was controlled by one – the wind
My enemy, my friend

Don't walk on the grass use the sidewalk

My enemy?
How could this be?
Enemy and friend – One
Flesh and Spirit – One
Trapped in Adam's relationship

## Your Eye

*"He found him in a desert land, and in the waste howling wilderness; he led him about, he instructed him, he kept him as the apple of his eye."*
Deuteronomy 32:10(KJV)

I look to the moon
And I say "I'll see you soon."
I see your people going through trials and tribulations
Yet you still save us out of all situations
I look to you for help and guidance
In your Word I find my insurance
I understand I love you and you love me

Your grace, mercy, and forgiveness led me out of captivity
I enjoy being your servant, your slave
I don't understand why your life you gave
I sinned and sinned
But you knew this and sent me a friend
A Comforter of joy and peace
Now you are my shepherd and I your sheep
I will follow your path, your way
I will be an example of you from day to day
I am your ministry, your foot soldier
I will be yours till my life is older
And then I will praise and worship you even more
My prayers, my praise, my worship, and my devotion you will never ignore
I look to the sky
And I yearn to be the apple of your eye

## Your Life

*"He that findeth his life shall lose it: and he that loseth his life for my sake shall find it."*
Matthew 10:39(KJV)

My life is your life, completely, completely
My life is your life, completely, completely

I'll follow you till the end of time
I know that you will provide
You are my glory and shield
Through your word I know your will

My life is your life, completely, completely
My life is your life, completely, completely

Without your love I will not be
With you there is no me
You give me my purpose and gifts
You living through me is my only wish

My life is your life, completely, completely
My life is your life, completely, completely

I give you me
Your truth gives me liberty
Your word I put my faith in
My praise and worship, you can put your faith in
You make a difference in my life
You take my burdens and strife
And make everything alright

My life is your life, completely, completely
My life is your life, completely, completely

I am you
I live through you
And you shine through me

My life is your life, completely, completely
My life is your life, completely, completely
My life is your life, completely, completely
My life is your life, completely, completely

My life was never mine
My life was never mine
My life was never mine
My life was never mine


## Salesman II
*"It was meet that we should make merry, and be glad: for this thy brother was dead,*
*and is alive again; and was lost, and is found."*
Luke 15:32(KJV)


As we continued to embrace
Tears fell down my face
With each tear I felt the pain
Hurt that would cause me to restrain
From being who God wanted me to be

Hurt not allowing me to see
Hurt that told me I was never good enough
End my life cause life is too tough
You're a failure, never going to amount to nothing
As each tear rolled down my pain had less sting
It was as if He was absorbing it all
But yet He still stood tall
Arms around me not letting go, why?
The more I thought about this the more I begin to cry

He whispered in my ear "I am Jesus and I came to give you something."
It was as if that statement answered everything
I felt so light
I could've become a bird in flight
I did not comprehend his purpose
What gift, why me, me and Him weren't even close
I didn't know Him from Nat Turner
But yet He was destined to be in my corner
I blurted out "I'm sorry, I was wrong, I'm wretched!!"
He would no longer be rejected
My life of ignoring Him has ended
The time of giving Him everything has been initiated

www.ingramcontent.com/pod-product-compliance
Lightning Source LLC
Chambersburg PA
CBHW021120020426
42331CB00004B/565